A few seeds, a little soil, a ray of sunshine,

a splash of rain, a breath of air—

this is Earth's recipe for the food we eat.

SEED SOIL SUN

Earth's Recipe for Food

Cris Peterson

photographs by
David R. Lundquist

BOYDS MILLS PRESS
Honesdale, Pennsylvania

To Ben and Nicki

—CP

To my daughters, Janna and Hilary,
who keep Dad smiling and happy!

—DL

Author Acknowledgments

I wish to extend gratitude and appreciation for expert readings of this text to
Professor Deborah L. Allan, Department of Soil, Water, and Climate,
University of Minnesota, St. Paul, and to
Alan Bertelsen, professional agronomist with
Winfield Solutions, LLC, A Land O'Lakes Company, Shoreview, Minnesota.

Text copyright © 2010 by Cris Peterson
Photographs copyright © 2010 by David R. Lundquist
Boyds Mills Press
An Imprint of Highlights
815 Church Street
Honesdale, Pennsylvania 18431
Printed in China

ISBN: 978-1-59078-713-7 (hc) • ISBN: 978-1-59078-947-6 (pb)

Library of Congress Control Number: 2010925652

First edition
Book design by Amy Drinker, Aster Designs

10 9 8 7 6 5 4 3

Nearly all of our food comes from seeds planted in the soil, moistened by the rain, and warmed by the sun. Tomatoes, potatoes, peppers, and peas all begin as tiny seeds. Apples, pineapples, melons, and mangoes start with seeds, too.
In fact, almost all plants on Earth grow from seeds.

Each spring farmers plant millions and millions of seeds in the soil, wait for good rains and warm sunshine, then watch their fields turn into food for harvest in the fall. Some crops grow into food for people, and some are fed to animals. Then the animals provide us with milk, meat, eggs, and other products.

More corn seeds are planted each year in the United States than any other kind of seed. Whether it is sweet corn in a backyard garden, field corn in a section of land that measures a mile across, or popcorn in a big bowl, it all begins with a little seed.

The beginning of a new plant is curled up inside each seed. Moisture from the rain filters down to the buried corn seed, softening its skin and causing it to swell and split open. Part of the seed—the root—grows down into the soil. Another part of the seed—the shoot—reaches for the sun.

A corn seed doesn't seem like much, but look out! When it
is placed in good soil and the sun shines and the rain falls,
the seed germinates, or sprouts. It takes only a few weeks
for the sprout to turn into a gigantic corn plant with roots
reaching down over six feet into the ground.

Soil is another ingredient needed to make food. This tiny layer of our Earth is made up of silt, sand, and clay, along with minerals, dead leaves, twigs, and a zillion tiny organisms. Each handful of soil contains more living things than all the human beings on Earth.

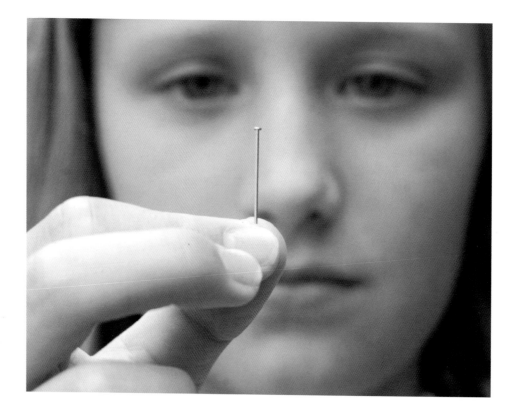

Microscopic one-celled bacteria that munch away on dead leaves and insects in the soil are so minute that it would take a thousand of them lined up in a row to reach across the head of a pin. They use the energy stored in the leaves, roots, twigs, and insects—recycling nutrients that feed the corn. The earthy odor of rich soil is bacteria at work.

Earthworms, amoebas, mites, and moles also live in the soil. As they search for food, earthworms slither through the dirt, eating debris and discharging it as a rich natural fertilizer called castings. They leave behind an underground network of tunnels that allows air and water to filter in. The air and water help the plant roots breathe and grow.

The soil provides a home for the seed, but the seed only has enough energy inside it to push the new seedling out of the soil. Then the sun takes over. Sunlight is a key ingredient in Earth's food recipe. Plants are the only living things that can use the sun's energy to grow.

Plant leaves are nature's food factories. Cells within the leaves absorb energy from sunlight, carbon dioxide from the air, and water through the plant's roots. Then these ingredients combine in a chemical reaction that creates sugar for the plant to grow and releases oxygen into the air for people to breathe.

The way plants turn sunlight, water, and carbon dioxide into sugar is called photosynthesis. And plants are really good at it. In fact, when they make energy, they make more than they need. They store the extra energy in their leaves, stems, flowers, fruits, roots, and seeds—our food from plants.

When you eat lettuce, you are eating a leaf.

When you eat celery, you are eating a stem.

When you eat broccoli, you are eating flower buds.

When you eat apples or tomatoes, you are eating fruits.

When you eat carrots, you are eating roots.

When you eat sweet corn, you are eating seeds.

And when you drink milk from a cow,

you are drinking a food made when the

cow eats plants like grass, corn, and soybeans.

All these foods begin as seeds. The seed starts the plant. The soil feeds the plant. The sun, the air, and the rain combine to grow the plant into food. And as they grow, all of Earth's plants produce oxygen for us to breathe. When the plants are harvested, they provide food for the world and new seeds to begin the cycle once again.

FURTHER READING

Dirt: Jump into Science by Steve Tomecek (National Geographic Society, 2002)

Dirt: The Scoop on Soil by Natalie M. Rosinsky (Picture Window Books, 2003)

From Seed to Plant by Gail Gibbons (Holiday House, 1991)

A Handful of Dirt by Raymond Bial (Walker, 2000)

How a Seed Grows by Helene J. Jordan (HarperCollins, 1992)

Life in a Bucket of Soil by Alvin Silverstein (Dover, 2000)

Living Sunlight: How the Sun Gives Us Life by Molly Bang and Penny Chisholm (Blue Sky Press, 2009)

Photosynthesis: Changing Sunlight into Food by Bobbie Kalman (Crabtree, 2005)

Roots Shoots Buckets & Boots: Gardening Together with Children by Sharon Lovejoy (Workman, 1999)

A Seed Is Sleepy by Dianna Hutts Aston (Chronicle, 2007)

Seeds by Ken Robbins (Atheneum, 2005)

SOURCES

Fundamentals of Soil Science by H.D. Foth (Wiley, 1990)

The Nature and Properties of Soils by Nyle C. Brady and Ray R. Weil (Pearson Prentice Hall, 2008)

Photosynthesis by D.W. Lawlor (Garland Science, 2000)

Principles of Field Crop Production by John H. Martin, Richard P. Waldren, and David L. Stamp (Pearson Prentice Hall, 2006)

Teaming with Microbes: A Gardener's Guide to the Soil Food Web by Jeff Lowenfels and Wayne Lewis (Timber Press, 2006)